Diana

Collecting the Princess

By Charles Nobles

Photographs by Clifford Hunt

Published by  Hobby House Press, Inc.
Grantsville, MD 21536

Dedication

To my mother, Flora Mae, for all her love and support and for starting my collection. To my late father, Enoch, for his love and support and for taking me to see Diana for the first time.

Acknowledgements

To my sister, Mary Lee, for her love and for being my best friend and travel companion.
To Shaun for the computer help and for being the brother I never had.
To Pat for her support and knowing what to say and how I felt on August 31, 1997.
To Scott for the friendship and the many mailings and all things "Angelic".
To Cliff for his photographs and his time.
To Charlotte Doyle and her staff at Newstand International in Charlotte, N.C.
To David for his support and encouragement and for an endless supply of stamps.
And to Diana for her strength and compassion and for making a difference.

Additional copies of this book may be purchased at $14.95 (plus postage & handling) from

HOBBY HOUSE PRESS, INC.

1 Corporate Drive
Grantsville, Maryland 21536

1-800-554-1447

or from your favorite bookstore or dealer.

ISBN: 0-87588-543-8

Table of Contents

About this book

This book contains a collection that I started in 1981. Each person who collects has things that they like better than others, and everyone's collection will be different and varied. Each item has been given a letter indicating the approximate value as follows:

A = $0-20	D = $76-150	G = $501+
B = $21-50	E = $151-350	
C = $51-75	F = $351-500	

The top value of each item lies within the price range of the letter it has been assigned. To determine the value, the following factors were taken into consideration: (1) current market demand, (2) availability, (3) rarity, and (4) varying dealer prices and author's personal experience. The values assigned are for information purposes only.

Condition

The condition of an item greatly influences its worth. Coloring books were colored in, paper dolls cut, etc. Heavy wear, defacement and soiling all reduce the value of such items considerably.

Chapter 1

Princess of Covers

Diana was without a doubt the most photographed woman of our generation. Hundreds of thousands of photographs were taken of her every move.

Those photographs landed on the cover of nearly every magazine imaginable, from *People* to *Soap Opera Digest* and even *TV Guide*, which had her on its cover five times.

Diana and *People* had a strong connection, and the magazine traces her life from her engagement to her death. She appeared somewhere on their cover almost 80 times, and five of those were after her death.

Diana understood the power of a picture, and in the last years of her life used them to highlight her causes and marital problems.

Women felt a strong bond with Diana, which explains her many *McCalls*, *Ladies Home Journal*, and *Good Housekeeping* covers. She had many of their same problems, and women understood her plight.

Foreign magazines play a major role in this collection; Spanish, Dutch, German, French, and the majority from her native Britain. *Majesty* and *Royalty* were virtually started to satisfy the need to know more about Diana, and it is not a coincidence that both began production in 1981. And one can only wonder if they can survive after her death.

This collection of magazines is by no means complete, and will continue to grow over the years, but it represents 16 years of love and collection on the Princess of Covers.

Top to bottom, left to right: *People*: 06-22-81: Lady Diana, (B); 08-03-81: Good Show, (B); 07-05-82: Oh Boy!, (B); 09-06-83: 30 Best & Worst Dressed People, (A); 01-31-83: Diana's Ordeal, (A); 10-01-84: Di's Pride and Joy, (A); 01-14-85: Harry, (A); 05-20-85: Talk About Power Trips, (A).

Top to bottom, left to right: *People*: 07-22-85: Malice in the Palace, (A); 11-11-85: What's Diana Worth to Britain?, (A); 07-07-86: Prince William Goes to Work, (A); 10-13-86: Fergie & Di-The Merry Wives of Windsor, (A), 06-08-87: Save the Wales, (A); 07-20-87: Naughty, Naughty, (A); 11-09- 87: The Big Chill, (A); 12-28-87/ 01-04-88: 25 Most Intriguing People of '87, (A).

Top to bottom, left to right: *People*: 04-25-88: Growing Up Royal, (A); 08-01-88: Seven Year Hitch, (A), September 1988: 10th Annual Reader's Poll, (A); 09-31-88: Life Without Di, (A); Fall 1989: The 80's, (A); 12-11-89: Best & Worst Dressed of 1989, (A); 07-16-90: The Woman Who Will Be Queen, (A); 02-11-91: Home Alone, (A).

Top to bottom, left to right: *People*: 06-17-91: Wounded Prince, (A); 07-22-91: Where Has Their Love Gone?, (A); 04-13-92: Diana in Mourning, (A); 06-22-92: Diana, (B); 06-29-92: Diana's Rival, (B); 08-03-92: Diana's Diet Ordeal, (A); 09-14-92: Diana's Secrets, (A); 10-26-92: Best & Worst Dressed '92, (A).

Top to bottom, left to right: *People*: 11-30-92: It's Over, (A); 12-21-92: Diana Makes a Deal, (A); 12-28-92 / 01-04-93: 25 Most Intriguing People of '92, (A); 04-12-93: Diana On Her Own, (A); 07-26-93: Here Come the Brides!, (A); 09-26-93: Battle for the Boys, (A); 10-25-93: Best & Worst Dressed '93, (A); 12-06-93: Diana's Lonely Battle, (A).

Top to bottom, left to right: *People*: 12-21-93/01-03-94: 25 Most Intriguing People of '93, (A); 06-13-94: Diana's Daring New Life, (A); 09-5-94: Diana on the Edge, (A); 09-19-94: Best & Worst Dressed of '94, (A); 10-17-94: Diana's Secret Lover, (A); 10-31-94: He Never Loved Her, (A); 12-26-94/1-02-95: 25 Most Intriguing People of '94, (A), 04-24-95: All Grown Up, (A).

Top to bottom, left to right: *People*: 11-06-95: Diana & Camilla, (A); 12-04-95: Diana's Revenge: Take That!, (A); 12-25-95/1-01-96: 25 Most Intriguing People of '95, (A); 03-11-96: Di-vorce!, (A); 06-17-96: Di Wows Chicago, (A); 03-17-97: Class vs. Cash, (A); 08-25-97: A Guy For Di, (B); 09-15-97: Diana's Death, (B).

Top to bottom, left to right: *People*: 09-22-97: Goodbye, Diana, (B); 10-20-97: The Diana Interviews, (A); 12-01-98: How They're Coping, (A); 12-29-98/01-05-98: 25 Most Intriguing People of '97, (A); 02-20-98: Diana's Legacy of Love, (A).

Top to bottom, left to right: *People*: Spring 1988: All About Diana, (B); Fall 1990: The Decade of Diana, (A); Private Lives 1993, (A); Spring 1996: The Diana Years, (B); The Diana Years, hardback, 1996, (B); Fall 1997: Diana, Princess of Wales 1961-1997, (A); The Diana Years Photo Special 1996, (B).

Top to bottom, left to right: *Time*: 04-20-81: The Prince's Charmer, (B); 08-03-81: Three Cheers, (B); 02-28-83: Royalty vs. the Press, (B); 11-11-89: Here They Come!, (A); 11-30-92: A House Dividing, (A); 03-11-96: It's Over, (A); 09-8-97: Special Report: Diana 1961-1997, (B); 9-15-97: Commemorative Issue, (B); 12-22-97: Images of '97, (A).

Top to bottom, left to right: *Newsweek*: 08-03-81: Royal Wedding, (B); 09-28-85: Guess Who's Coming to Dinner, (A); 06-22-92: Private Lives, (A); 12-21-92: On Her Own, (A); 12-04-95: Why She Won't Go Away, (A); 03-11-96: Royal Split, (A); 09-08-97: Princess Diana 1961-1997, (B); Commemorative Issue 1997, (A); 12-22-97: Pictures of the Year, (A).

Top to bottom, left to right: *Life*: January 1982: The Year in Pictures, (B); December 1982: Princess Di is Back, (B); December 1984: Diana And The Newest Star In The Royal Family, (B); November 1985: A Royal Welcome, (B); Fall 1989: The 80's, (B).

Top to bottom, left to right: *Life*: August 1992: Diana: What Happened and Why, (A); January 1993: Year in Pictures '92, (A); February 1993: Once Upon a Time, (A); November 1997: Diana: Portrait of a Lady, (A); December 1997: Year in Pictures '97, (A); Year in Pictures (paperback), (A).

Top to bottom, left to right: *Vanity Fair*: October 1985: Mouse that Roared, (B); September 1988: Diana: Brought to Heel?, (B), February 1993: Di's Palace Coup, (A); August 1997: Diana: Auction Dresses, (C). *British Heritage*: 02-3-86: Treasure Houses of Britain, (B); 10-11-94: Royalty Remembers, (A); December 1997/Janaury 1998: Diana's Role in History, (B).

Top to bottom, left to right: *Us*: 06-18-82: Royal Baby, (A); 04-09-84: Pregnant Princesses, (A); 12-16-85: The Di-Namic Duo, (B); 11-16-87: Di-ing for Attention, (A). *European Travel & Life*: 07-08-89: The New Diana, (A); 06-07-90: The Natural, (B).

Top to bottom, left to right: *Good Housekeeping*: February 1982: Joys & Problems of Being Charles' Wife, (B); February 1983: My 12 Years with Prince Charles, (A); April 1984: Never Before Stories, (A); February 1985: Upstairs at the Palace, (A); November 1986: At-Home Exclusive, (A); June 1987: Look Inside Diana's Closet, (B); November 1987: Year of the Royal Mess, (A); May 1988: Solving the Puzzle of Diana's Marriage, (A); August 1993: What's Next for Charles & Diana, (A).

Top to bottom, left to right: *McCall's*: June 1982: Princess Diana, (A); August 1983: The Lady Di Look, (B); March 1984: Facing the Terrible Twos & Baby No. 2, (A); July 1984: Princess Diana: My New Baby, (A); March 1985: Good-Bye, Shy Di!, (A); August 1985: Princess Di's Hair Stylist, (A).

Top to bottom, left to right: *McCall's*: November 1987: Di & Fergie, (A); June 1989: Diana: Secrets of Her Style, (A); October 1990: Diana's Tough Decision, (B); June 1991: Can Diana Hold On?, (A); February 1993: Diana's New Life, (A); March 1994: Diana's Life Alone, (A); April 1995: Diana's Sweet Revenge, (A).

Top to bottom, left to right: *Ladies' Home Journal*: February 1982: Dazzling Diana, (B); June 1983: Diana: The Palace Answers Your Questions, (B); October 1983: LHJ Goes to a Ball with Diana, (A); July 1984: Diana: How the New Baby Will Change Her Life, (A); November 1985: Inside the Court of Princess Diana, (A); July 1987: Diana: Super Photos of Her and the Newest Princess, (A); July 1987: Diana & Charles, (A).

Top to bottom, left to right: *Ladies' Home Journal*: February 1988: Diana: Her Secret Life; July 1988: Diana: What She Does Better Than Anyone; February 1989: Diana & Charles, (A); August 1989: Is Diana Happy?, (A); February 1990: Diana's Darlings, (A); June 1991: Diana Ten Years Later, (A); August 1993: Diana Today, (A).

Top to bottom, left to right: *Dossier*: November 1985: Title Wave Hits Town, (C); *WJR*: November 1985: Royal Family Meets the Press, (B); *U.S. News*: 9-15-97: After Diana, (A); *Chicago*: August 1996: DiConfidential, (A); *Spy*: November 1991: What Year is it, Anyway?, (A); *Celebrity Hairstyles*: August 1988: Princess Di: Her Chic Glamour Style, (B); *Entertainment Weekly*: 9-17-97: Diana's Death, (A); *British Airways Highlife*: July 1985: London Style, (B).

Top to bottom, left to right: *Cover*: March 1998: Can't Live Without You, (A); *In Style*: February 1994: Secrets of Personal Style, (B); *Longevity*: July 1992: Diana: Surviving Stress and Scandal, (A); *Fitness*: January/February 1996: Princess Di's Workout Plan, (A); *A & E Monthly*: August 1996: Royal Splitsville!, (A); *New Woman*: After the Crisis, A New Woman Emerges, (A); *The Saturday Evening Post*: June/July 1981: A Royal Romance, (A); September 1989: A Day With Diana, (A).

Top to bottom, left to right: *Harper's Bazaar*: December 1995: Her Royal Highness The Princess of Wales, (B); *Woman's World*: 11-22-89: Is Di too hot for her cold fish prince?, (A); 02-27-90: Diana's Beauty Secrets, (A); *Harper's Bazaar*: November 1997: A Tribute to a Princess, (B); *Woman's World*: 01-21-89: Diana's Dirt, (A); 09-22-92: What Diana and Charles can still do to save their marriage; 02-7-95: Diana: Her new life, Her new look, (A).

Top to bottom, left to right: *Celebrity*: January 1988: Queen Says No to Divorce, (B); March 1988: The Mystery Man in Di's Life, (B); *First for Women*: 08-30-92: Charles and Di: How Will It End?, (A); 10-19-92: Malice in the Palace, (B); *Confetti*: June/July 1990: Royal Jealousy, (C); Collecting Figures: February 1998 – A World of Good, (A); *Fame*: Diana: Royal Problems?, (C); *Vogue*: Princess Diana: Leading Royalty into Reality, (B);

Top to bottom, left to right: *TV Guide*: July 25-31, 1981: The Royal Wedding, (B); November 9-15, 1985: Charles and Diana, (A); May 21-27, 1988: This Week: A Royal Gala, (A); August 8-14, 1992: Di vs. Chuck: The Soap Opera, (B); September 20-26, 1997: Princess Diana, (A); *Soap Opera Digest*: 09-1-92: Britain's Real-Life Soap, (B); *American Photo*: 100 Most Important People in Photography, (A); *Astrologer*: October 1989: Diana's Royal Horoscope, (A).

Top to bottom, left to right: *British Vogue*: July 1994: The Princess of Wales: New Portraits, (B); October 1997: 1961-1997, (B); *Hello/Hola*: 01-04-97: Princess Diana at Christmas, (B); 04-12-97: Diana: Trapped Between Two Worlds, (B); 07-05-97: Diana & Christopher Whalley, (A); 06-14-97: Diana: A Woman of Contrasts, (B); 07-10-97: New York Gala, (B); 07-26-97: Diana: Making Waves, (B); 09-06-97: The World Mourns Diana, Princess of Wales, (C).

Top to bottom, left to right: *O.K.!* (British): Vol. 1 #5: Princess Diana, (A); *Paris Match* (French): 07-10-87: Lady Di Infidele?; 03-06-87: Diana & Sarah, (A); 05-11-87: L'ete Dore Des Princesses, (A); 10-13-94: Exclusive: James Hewitt, (A); 11-12-95: Diana Ca Suffit!, (A); 11-30-95: Diana A Nu, (B); 03-14-96: Diana libre, (B).

Top to bottom, left to right: *Paris Match* (French): 07-29-97: Diana: A Saint Tropez, (A); 09-11-97: 1961-1997 Un Destin; 12-25-97: Diana & Dodi, (B); 06-11-98: L'accident de Diana, (A); *Tattler*: August 1990: Di laughing, (A); April 1993: Diana: Who Will She Marry Next?, (B); December 1993: Diana: monster or martyr?, (B); December 1994: Diana: where do you go to now my lovely?, (A).

Top to bottom, left to right: *Point De Vue* (French): 10-24-95: Diana, Caroline, Stephanie, (A); 11-28-95: Diana Elle A Ose!, (A); 01-02-96: Que Va Devemir Diana, (A); 04-08-97: Diana en quere avec, (A); 03-11-97: Diana vend ses robes, (A); *Bunte* (Germany): 04-07-96: bei Lady Di zu Hause, (A); 05-30-96: Warum wahlte Diana, (A).

Top to bottom, left to right: Das Neue Blatt (German): 12-17-96: Diana und ihr Herzchirurg, (A); 12-23-96: Diana & Sarah, (A); 01-15-97: Diana: ihre Marchenhochzeit, (A); 01-03-97: Diana Die Scheidungsschlacht, (A); 02-21-97: Diana: Jetzt kauft sie das, (A); 02-05-97: Gluckliche Diana, (A); 04-02-97: Diana Schwanger, (A); 04-23-97: Grober Triumph! Diana, (A).

Top to bottom, left to right: Das Neue Blatt (German): 06-25-97: Diana: der offizielle, (A); 07-14-97: Diana & Charles; 07-02-97: Diana ich wunsche mir noch ein Baby!, (A); *Frau im Spiegel* (Dutch): 10-12-96: Diana Funf Manner, (A); 04-18-96: Diana Die gefahrllchem, (A); 11-02-96: Dianas Kampf, (A); 05-23-96: Wie Reich ist Diana?, (B); 10-10-96: Diana Gefahrliches Spiel um Liebe, (A).

Top to bottom, left to right: *Frau im Spiegel* (Dutch): 08-07-97: Diana für den Mann, (A); 05-22-97: Bulimie Diana, (A); *A* (Danish): 11-25-95: Diana's TV-Beichte, (A); 06-30-97: Diana die Bose Luge, (B); 09-18-97: Diana in Seelennot, (A); 09-11-97: Diana Sensations-Fotos!, (A); *Das Neue* (Danish): 07-08-95: Das Drama um das Baby, (A); 04-26-96: Diana Herzoperation!, (A).

Top to bottom, left to right: *Das Neue* (Danish): 01-13-96: Diana Sie glaubte, (A); 12-22-95: Diana und ihren neuen fruund, (A); 06-07-97: ihre söhne wenden, (A); 08-09-97: Diana ihre neue grobe Liebe, (A); Neue Post *(Danish):* 11-23-95: Dianas sensationelle Fernsehbeichte, (A); 05-30-96: Diana en Juan Carlos, (A); 06-13-97: Diana und Steffi Graf im Netz der Intrigen, (A); 06-27-96: Ring von Charles, (A).

Top to bottom, left to right: *Neue Post*: 07-11-96: Was Prince William über die, (A); 07-03-97: Dianas Triumph, (B); 5-28-97: Charles Nebenfrau Camilla, (A); 09-04-97: Tiefe Trauer um Prinzessin Diana, (B); 06-04-98: Diana mit ihren Sohnen, (A); *Freizeit Revue* (Danish): 10-31-97: Peinliche Nacht mit, (A); 01-03-96: Diana und der, (A); 02-21-96: Opfer oder Taterin?, (A).

Top to bottom, left to right: *Paranoia*: Vol. 5 No. 3: Diana, Magic, and Ritual Murder, (A); *British Esquire*: November 1994: The Princess Always Rings Twice, (C); *Freizeit Revue* (Danish): 06-12-96: Diana und die Hewitt-Uberraschung, (A); 07-24-96: Diana's Tranen, (A); 07-31-96: Diana und der Junse Kennedy, (A); 01-15-97: Hat Diese Liebe, (A); *Chi* (Italy): 05-09-97: I figli di Diane e Carolina, (B); 06-06-97: Diana diventa modella, (B); 08-22-97: Sexy Diana per amore, (B); *Vanidades* (Spanish): July 1995: Diana enfrenta a Camilla, (B); August 1996: Reina de los corazones, (B).

Top to bottom, left to right: *Majesty* (Britain): Vol. 4 No. 7: How Diana has Adapted to Married Life, (B); Vol. 4 No. 11: Princess of Wales Goes it Alone, (B); Vol. 5 No. 3: Princess of Wales Birthday Look, (B); Vol. 5 No. 6: Cheers for Diana, (B); Vol. 5 No. 7: Prince Harry in Focus, (B); Vol. 5 No. 8: Diana & The Princess of Wales, (B); Vol. 6 No. 11: Living Thru a Lens, (B); Vol. 6 No. 8: On Tour with Charles and Diana, (B).

Top to bottom, left to right: *Majesty* (Britain): Vol. 7 No. 2: Diana and Sarah: Palace Pals, (B); Vol. 7 No. 6: Diana, William and Harry on Holiday, (B); Vol. 7 No. 10: The Price of Popularity for Diana, (B); Vol. 7 No. 12: Alpine Sports, (A); Vol. 8 No. 2: Spanish Eyes on Diana and Charles, (B); Vol. 8 No. 4: Royal Summer Season, (B); Vol. 8 No. 6: Holidays & Hobbies, (B); Vol. 8 No. 8: Private Lives on Public View, (B).

Top to bottom, left to right: *Majesty* (Britain): Vol. 8 No. 12: Seeing Red-Diana's Style, (A); Vol. 9 No. 3: Finally The Truth Is Out, (B); Vol. 9 No. 6: Sealed with Approval, (B); Vol. 9 No. 8: Diana at Home and Abroad, (B); Vol. 9 No. 9: Diana, Caroline, & Stephanie, (B); Vol. 9 No. 11: Uptown Still – Diana in New York, (A); Vol. 10 No. 3: Diana, the Making of a Queen, (B); Vol. 10 No. 6: Charles & Diana: Their Secret Loves, (B).

Top to bottom, left to right: *Majesty* (Britain): Vol. 10 No. 7: Charles at Ul, (A); Vol. 10 No. 9: The Carling Tour, (B); Vol. 11 No. 5: 10th Anniversary Issue, (C); Vol. 11 No. 7: Diana's Eternal Flame, (B); Vol. 11 No. 11: Secrets of the Royal Wardrobe, (B); Vol. 12 No. 1: Interview with Diana's Father, (B); Vol. 12 No. 6: A Decade of Diana, (B); Vol. 12 No. 12: Family Fun in Canada, (B).

Top to bottom, left to right: *Majesty* (Britain): Vol. 13 No. 1: Pictures of the Year, (B); Vol. 13 No. 4: Charles & Diana in India, (B); Vol. 13 No 6: Diana's Life, (B); Vol. 13 No. 7: Diana Sets the Pace For Social Season, (B); Vol. 13 No. 8: Marriage & the Monarchy, (B); Vol. 13 No. 9: All Together Now, (B); Vol. 13 No. 10: Diana's Dilemma, (B); Vol. 13 No. 12: Diana and Her Boy Racers, (B).

Top to bottom, left to right: *Majesty* (Britain): Vol. 14 No. 1: Charles & Diana: Separate Lives, (C); Vol. 14 No. 2: Diana in the Caribbean, (B); Vol. 14 No. 3: Diana's Health Secrets, (B); Vol. 14 No. 5: Diana Confronts the Press in Austria, (B); Vol. 14 No. 12: What is Happening to the Princess of Wales?, (B); Vol. 15 No. 2: Starting Over, (B); Vol. 15 No. 3: Diana's New Style, (B); Vol. 15 No. 5: Diana's Fight for a Private Life, (B).

Top to bottom, left to right: *Majesty* (Britain): Vol. 15 No. 9: Diana's Troubled Childhood, (B); Vol. 15 No. 11: Diana's Men & Charles' Women, (B); Vol. 16 No. 1: It's A Scandal, (B); Vol. 16 No. 3: Diana's New Man, (A); Vol. 16 No. 4: Diana's Mother: A Life in Exile, (A); Vol. 16 No. 9: Is This Diana's Rival?, (A); Vol. 16 No. 11: Defending Diana, (A); Vol. 17 No. 1: The Tender Trap, (A).

Top to bottom, left to right: *Majesty* (Britain): Vol. 17 No. 2: The Long Goodbye, (A); Vol. 17 No. 5: Free Spirit, (A); Vol. 17 No. 7: The Great Escape, (A); Vol. 17 No. 9: The New Diana, (B); Vol. 17 No. 11: Queen of the USA, (B); Vol. 17 No. 12: The Fame Game, (A); Vol. 18 No. 2: Secret Life, (A); Vol. 18 No. 5: The Ultimate Collection, (B); Commemorative Issue, (B); Vol. 19 No. 3: Snow Princess, (A); Royal Year 1991, (B).

NO. 1 JULY 1981 60p

Royalty MONTHLY

LADY
DIANA'S
FAMILY ALBUM

WIN A
£250
STERLING
SILVER
ROYAL WEDDING BELL

WHAT MUST
WE DO TO
PROTECT
OUR ROYAL FAMILY?

WEDDING COMMEMORATIVE OFFER INSIDE

Royalty Monthly, Premiere Issue, Vol. 1 No. 1: One of Diana's first magazine covers, (B-C).

Top to bottom, left to right: *Royalty Monthly* (Britain): No. 2: Charles & Diana's Great Day in Colour, (B); Vol. 2 No. 12: Who's a Little Superstar Then?, (B); Vol. 4 No. 6: Diana on the Road Again, (B); Vol. 4 No. 7: Diana's New Look, (B); Vol. 4 No. 12: Che Bella!, (B); Vol. 5 No. 4: Can Diana Knock 'Em Dead, (A); Vol. 6 No. 5: Royal Fashion Watch, (A); Vol. 6 No. 6: Diana: A Fresh Look in the Camera, (A).

Top to bottom, left to right: *Royalty Monthly* (Britain): Vol. 6 No. 9: Diana Ole!, (B); Vol. 6 No. 11: Charles & Diana, (B); Vol. 7 No. 5: The Diana Years, (B); Vol. 7 No. 7: Royal Ski Tragedy, (B); Vol. 7 No. 8: How Diana Gets That Dazzle, (A); Vol. 7 No. 11: Diana's Dilemma, (B); Vol. 8 No. 4: French Dressing, (B); Vol. 8 No. 6: Diana, Belle of New York, (A).

Top to bottom, left to right: *Royalty Monthly* (Britain): Vol. 8 No. 1: Modern Mother, (A); Vol. 8 No. 8: Diana's Dilemma, (A); Vol. 8 No. 9: Royal Godmother, (A); Vol. 9 No. 2: Dressing Up for Britain, (A); Vol. 9 No. 3: East Meets West, (B); Vol. 9 No. 4: 100 Anniversary Issue, (B); Vol. 9 No. 6: Here's Lookin' at You Kid, (A); Vol. 9 No. 9: Charles & Diana in Hungary, (B).

Top to bottom, left to right: *Royalty Monthly* (Britain): Vol. 10 No. 4: Does This Man Have Designs on Diana?, (A); Vol. 10 No. 7: Staying Ahead: (A); Vol. 10 No. 9: The Children's Princess, (A); Vol. 11 No. 3: The Little Girl Who Called Diana Auntie, (B); Vol. 11 No. 9: Diana's Long Hot Summer, (B); Vol. 11 No. 11: Diana, At War With The Palace; Vol. 12 No. 1: The Truth Behind the Fairy Tale, (A); Vol. 12 No. 3: Diana: Solo Superstar, (A).

Top to bottom, left to right: *Royalty Monthly* (Britain): Vol. 12 No. 6: Diana: Saving the Monarchy, (B); Vol. 12 No. 7: The New Icon Diana, (B); Vol. 12 No. 10: Battle Royal, (B); Vol. 12 No. 12: Diana, Camilla, and Me, (B); Vol. 13 No. 2: Thirty Something, (B); Vol. 13 No. 3: Diana: The Decade of the Dream, (B); Vol. 13 No. 4: Diana Part II, (A); Vol. 13 No. 5: Divorce for Charles & Diana, (B).

Top to bottom, left to right: *Royalty Monthly* (Britain): Vol. 13 No. 6: Diana's Nightmare, (A); Vol. 13 No. 7: Diana's Worst Year, (B); Vol. 13 No. 8: Will Charles think the unthinkable?, (A); Vol. 13 No. 11: V.E. Day Celebrations, (A); Vol. 13 No. 12: Diana in Venice & Russia; Vol. 14 No. 5: Diana: A New Era, (A); Vol. 14 No. 7: Diana's Dilemma, (B); Vol. 14 No. 8: Diana: Life After Charles, (B).

Top to bottom, left to right: *Royalty Monthly* (Britain): Vol. 15 No. 1: Was Diana Murdered?, (B); Commemorative Issue, (B); Decade of Diana – Collector's Issue No. 1, (C), Mint; Charles & Diana Collector's Issue No. 4, (C), Mint; A Year of Royalty Collector's Issue No. 5, (B); *London News* Royal Issues: 1986, (C); 1987, (C); 1988, (B); 1991, (C).

Top to bottom, left to right: Collector's Edition – *Princess Diana* (1995), (B); *Diana: HRH The Princess of Wales* (Britain), 1991, (C); *Diana: The Real Story of Her Life,* 1991, (B); Gold Collector's Series: *Princess Di,* 1993, (B); *Royal Scandal,* 1992, (B); *Diana Portfolio,* 1991, (B); *Diana in her own words,* 1992, (B); *Princess Diana: A Royal Mother,* 1981, (B).

Top to bottom, left to right: *True Story* Diana Collector's Edition , 1992, (B); *OK* Special Issue, 1997, (C); *Tribute to Diana,* 1997, (B); *A Final Farewell,* 1997, (A); *Diana: Life of a Legend,* 1997, (A); *Diana: Royal Tribute,* 1997, (A); *Diana: The People's Princess,* 1997, (A); *Diana: Her Life in Words & Pictures,* 1997, (A).

Top to bottom, left to right: *A Tribute to Princess Diana,* 1997, (A); *Diana: The Palace Years,* 1997, (A); *A Celebration in her Memory,* 1998, (A); *A Personal Picture Album,* 1997, (A); *1st Anniversary Commemorative,* 1998, (A); *Miracles,* March 1995, Diana: Occult Obsession, (B).

Chapter 2

The Princess and the Book

Like magazines, Diana and books went hand in hand. In 1981 and 1982, no fewer than 50 books were published about her. Most of these were from Crescent or Colour Library and covered such subjects as the Royal Wedding and Charles and Diana's Royal Tours. Many of these books focused on Diana's fashions and featured the latest photos of her and the Royal Family, and were large coffee table books that were heavy on photos and light on reading.

In the last 17 years, more books have been written about Diana than have been written about the Queen and Prince Charles together in the last 30 years. Following Diana's death last August, a multitude of books hit the market. Some were better than others, and many were old books that were given new life with a new cover and title. One example is <u>Diana: Her Life in Photographs</u>, which was originally published in 1995 and reissued in 1997 as <u>Diana: A Tribute in Photographs</u>. Of all the books published after her death, two stand out as great ones: <u>Dressing Diana</u> and <u>Diana, Portrait of a Princess</u>. Both are well worth the money.

For the first anniversary of her death, no fewer than 17 books have been published to mark the event. And in years to come I am sure we will see many more as Diana will always enthrall and enchant readers.

Top to bottom, left to right: <u>Invitation to a Royal Wedding</u>, Crescent, 1981, (C); <u>Debrett's Book of the Royal Wedding</u>, Viking Press, 1981, (B); <u>The Country Life Book of Diana, Princess of Wales</u>, Crescent, 1981, (C); <u>Wedding Day</u>, Pikkin, 1981, (B); <u>A Day To Remember</u>, Crescent, 1981, (C); <u>Royal Wedding Album</u>, Beekman Books, 1981, (B).

Top to bottom, from left to right: Princess Diana Lady of Fashion, Crescent Books, 1982, (B); Princess, Times Books, 1981, (B); Charles And Diana's Tour Of North America, Crescent, 1983, (C); Diana, the Radiant Princess, Greenwich, 1983, (B); Charles & Diana, Crescent, 1982, (B); The Year Of The Princess, Little, Brown, 1982, (C).

Top to bottom, from left to right: Diana, Princess of Wales, Mother-to-be, Pitkin, 1982, (B); The Book of Fashion, Crescent, 1983, (C); Charles & Diana's First Royal Tour, 1983, (C); Diana, Princess of Wales, Greenwich House, 1983, (B); Diana, Princess of Wales, Holt Reinhart, 1983, (B); Born To Be King, Crescent, 1982, (B).

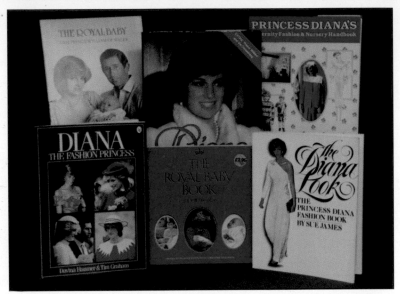

Top to bottom, from left to right: The Royal Baby, Pitkin, 1982, (B); Diana: A Celebration, 1982, (B); Princess Diana's Maternity Fashion & Nursery Handbook, Crescent, 1984, (B); Diana The Fashion Princess, Holt-Reinhart, 1984, (B); The Royal Baby Book, Octopus, 1984, (B); The Diana Look, Quill, 1984, (C).

Top to bottom, from left to right: Diana Her Latest Fashions, Crescent, 1984, (B); The Story of Diana, Greenwich House, 1984, (C); Prince Harry and the Royal Family, Crescent, 1984, (B); Royal Style Wars, Crescent, 1987, (B); Charles And Diana In America, Crescent, 1985, (B); Princess Diana's Latest Fashion Collection, Crescent, 1985, (B).

Top to bottom, from left to right: Charles & Diana — The First Five Yearss, Scott, 1986, (C); In Private-In Public, Crescent, 1986 (B); Charles & Diana – The Tenth Anniversary, 1991, (B); Charles & Diana: A Royal Family Album, Cresent, 1991, (B); In Person: The Prince And Princess Of Wales, Crescent, 1985, (B).

Top to bottom, from left to right: Diana H.R.H. The Princess of Wales, Michael O'Mara, 1991, with author autograph, (C); Diana Twentieth-Century Princess, 1986, (A); Illustrated Fashion Guide, Hardback, Michael Howard, with author autograph, (C); Diana, Her Life in Photographs, Michael O'Mara, 1995, (Reissued as Diana: A Tribute in 1997); Princess Diana – A True Fairy Tale, 1997, (B); Illustrated Fashion Guide (updated paperback), 1991, (B).

Top to bottom, from left to right: Dicing With Di, Blake, 1995, (B); Diana Princess of Wales, 1993, (B); The Making of a Queen, Gallery, 1995, (B); Diana's Diary, Simon and Schuster, 1990, (B); Diana – The Real Story of Her Private Life, 1991, (B); Diana, Princess of Wales, Scholastic, 1987, (B); Royal Fashion & Beauty Secrets, Villard, 1991, (B).

Top to bottom, from left to right: Diana, Princess of Wales, Bendford, 1997, (A); Diana, Portrait of a Princess, Callaway, 1998, (B); Dressing Diana, Bendford, 1998, (B); Diana: A Princess For The World, Barnes & Noble, 1997, (B); The People's Princess: A Memorial, Stewert, Tabor, Chams, 1997, (B); Her Life and Legacy, Random House, 1997, (B).

Top to bottom, from left to right: The Royal Family: A Year in Focus, Michael Joseph, 1985, (B); The Royal Year 1988, Summitt, 1989, (B); The Royal Year 1990, Summitt, 1991, (B); The Royal Year, Hold-Reinhart, 1984, (C); The Royal Year, Summitt, 1988, (B); The Royal Year – 1989, Summitt, 1990, (B).

Top to bottom, from left to right: The Royal Year 1991, Summitt, 1992, (B); The Royal Year 1993, Simon & Schuster, 1994, (B); The Royal Year, Crescent, 1995, (B); The Royal Year 1992, Simon & Schuster, 1993, (B).

Top to bottom, from left to right: Fall Of The House of Windsor, Contemporary, 1992, (B); Royal Style, St. Martins Press, 1986, (B); The Selling of the Royal Family, Simon & Schuster, 1986, (B); Charles & Diana, Putnam, 1985, (B); Diana – An Intimate Portrait, St. Martins, 1989, (B); The Definitive Diana, Contemporary, 1991, (B).

Top to bottom, from left to right: Diana – Her True Story (British), Michael O'Mara, 1992, (C); Diana – Her New Life, Simon & Schuster, 1994, (B); Diana – Her True Story (commemorative edition), Simon & Schuster, 1997, (B).

Top to bottom, from left to right: Death Of A Princess, St. Martins, 1997, (B); The Princess & The Package, 1998, (B); Diana – The Last Year, Harmony Books, 1997, (B); The Princess And The Duchess, St. Martins, 1989, (A); Diana — A Princess And Her Troubled Marriage, Birch Lane, 1992, (B); Behind Palace Doors, Putnam, 1992, (B); Diana – The Lonely Princess, Birch Lane, 1996, (B).

Top to bottom, from left to right: Famous Faces, Dorling Kindersley, 1995, (A); The Royal Family Pop-Up Book, Bounty, 1983, (C); The Official Sloane Ranger Handbook, Ebury Press, 1982, (B); "Not tonight darling, I've got a hairdo!", Sphere Books, 1986, (B); The Official Sloane Ranger Diary, Ebury Press, 1983, (B).

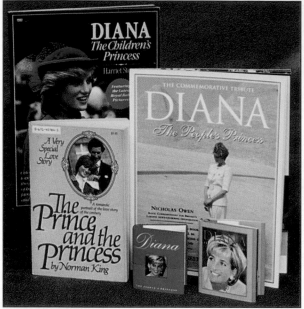

Diana – The Children's Princess, Fawcett, 1983, (A); Diana – The People's Princess, Reader's Digest, 1997, (A); The Prince and the princess, Walaby, 1981, (A); Diana – The People's Princess, Running Press, 1997, (A); Diana – The Life of a Princess, Ariel Books, 1997, (A).

Top to bottom, from left to right: Charles and Diana, Dell Paperback, 1982, (A); Royal Service, Avon Books, 1983, (A); Charles and Diana, Dell Paperback, 1981, (A); Royalty Revealed, St. Martins, 1992, (A); Diana – Her True Story, Pocket Books, 1992, (A); Diana In Private, St. Martins, 1992, (A); Diana vs. Charles: Royal Blood Feud, Signet, 1993, (A); With Love From Diana, Pocket, 1993, (A); Princess Diana — The Book of Love, Eagle Rose, 1997, (A); Royalty Watching, Fodores, 1992, (B); Diana – Her New Life, Pocket, 1994, (A); Diana – Queen of Hearts, Random House, 1997, (A).

Chapter 3

The Children's Princess

Before Diana was the People's Princess, she was the Children's Princess. Children always had a special place in her heart, and for the many children she met and held over the years she was a true princess. It is not surprising that there is a strong connection between Diana and children: toys.

Diana's likeness was immortalized in many dolls, although they were not very flattering most of the time. They range from BARBIE® styles with many outfits to wedding gowns that every little girl dreams about.

Also included in this chapter are puzzles, paper dolls and coloring books. These feature Diana at her most glamorous and in fashions that became part of her legacy.

Probably the most unusual item is the children's tape and book set that I discovered on a trip to London. I found it charming and unusual and added it proudly to my collection.

The last section of this chapter includes posters, something we don't normally associate with royalty. Some were put out after her death to help a grieving nation come to grips with its sorrow. A few came from my early years of collecting, and many I did myself when I didn't know what to do with all these extra pictures.

Left to right: "Lady Diana Spencer", 8-inch doll, Peggy Nisbet, 1981, (D); "Charles and Diana" Royal Wedding dolls, Peggy Nisbet, 1981, (D) each, (E) set; "Royal Baby Boy", Peggy Nisbet, Limited Edition 5000, 1982, (D); "The Royal Children", Peggy Nisbet, Limited Edition 1,000, 1984, (E).

Princess Diana Royal Wedding model, 14-inch vinyl, Peggy Nisbet Dolls, 1982, (D).

Princess Diana opening of Parliament gown, 14-inch vinyl, Peggy Nisbet Dolls, 1985 (D)

Princess Diana White House Gown, 14-inch vinyl, Peggy Nisbet, 1986, (D).

Princess Diana and Prince Charles wedding models, 1982, Diana (B), Charles (A), set (C).

Princess Diana in Hachi gown,
11-1/2 inches, 1984, (C).

Left to right: "Princess Diana Royal Wardrobe Collection", 11-1/2-inch doll and 24 fashions with accessories, Danbury Mint, 1988-1989, (E).

Left to right: Close-up of "Royal Wardrobe Collection" showing detail of fashions.

Close-up of 11-1/2-inch fashion doll in "Princess Diana Royal Wardrobe Collection", Diana wearing portrait gown, Danbury Mint, 1988.

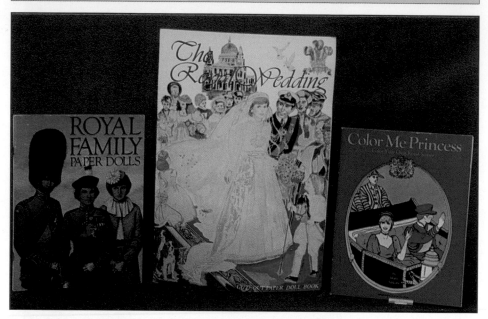

Left to right: "Royal Family Paper Dolls" and coloring book, 1982, (B); "The Royal Wedding" paper doll book, Courtier Art, 1981 (produced before wedding), (C); "Color Me Princess" coloring book, Dell, 1982, (C).

Left to right: "Princess Diana and Prince Charles" paper dolls, Dover, 1985, (B); "Diana, Princess of Wales" charity auction dresses paper dolls, Dover, 1997, (A); "Chuck & Di Have a Baby" paper dolls, Fireside Books, 1982, (B); "The Princess Diana Paper Doll Book of Fashion", Perigee Books, 1982, (C).

Left to right: "Princess Diana: Once Upon a Time" comic books, Topps, 1997, (B); <u>Where's Charles & Di?</u>, Ten Speed Press, 1992, (B); "Princess Diana Paper Doll", Golden Books, 1985, (B).

H.R.H. Princess of Wales 500-piece puzzle, 1991, (B).

Charles and Diana puzzle, 500 pieces, Waddington, 1986, (B).

Left to right: Royal Family trading cards, set of 100 in box, Press Pass, 1993, (B) (only Diana's cards are shown).

Left to right: Diana, Queen of Hearts trading cards, set of 50 in box, T.C.I. Inc., 1997, (B).

Diana tape and storybook, Tempo Story Time, 1986, (B); Princess magnetic dress-up, Ata-Boy, Inc., 1997, (B).

Royal Wedding magazine poster, 1981, (B).

Diana poster, made in the
U.K., 1984, (B).

The Australian Women's Weekly magazine promotional poster, 1993, (B).

Diana collage, made by the author, 1987, (A).

Harper's Bazaar poster, made by author, December, 1995, (A).

British promotional poster, Pyramid Inc., 1997, (B).

Diana Poster (1961 – 1997),
Funky Enterprises, (A).

Diana lyric poster, Funky
Enterprises, 1997, (A).

Diana photo mosaic, Robert Silvers, 1997, (B).

Barnes & Noble promotional flats, set of 2, 1997, (B).

Chapter 4

Sight and Sound

I remember finding the record album of Charles and Diana's wedding and thinking it was so cool. I was just beginning to collect, and was searching for items to add to my collection.

Over the years, videos of all sorts have been produced about Diana, proving further that she was a media princess of the media age. Her fashions, early life, motherhood, and her marriage have been the subject of the videos in this chapter. After her death, videos were produced that traced her life and death. Only one video, "Diana, the People's Princess", was authorized by her memorial fund and had the approval of her family.

Diana loved music, and over her lifetime attended several concerts and performances of her favorites. So it is not surprising that a tribute compact disc was released in her memory and included many of her favorite singers and performers. Her funeral was also released on compact disc, and after some concern did contain the Elton John tribute, which is the best-selling single in history. Probably the most complete compact disc is the two-disc set by the BBC, which includes her speeches and highlights of her life.

Over the years, I am certain Diana will continue to live on in videos, and her tribute CDs will keep her admirers comforted.

Royal Wedding record album, BBC Music, 1981, (C); Royal Wedding Official Souvenir, Pitkin, 1981, (B); postcards, Prescott, 1981.

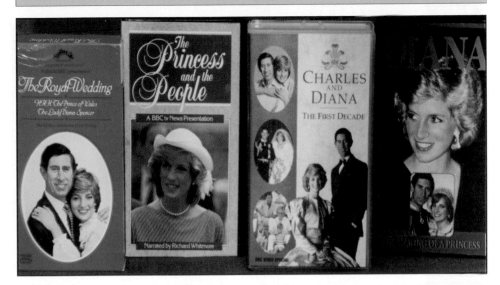

"The Royal Wedding", Trolley Car Video, 1981, (B); "The Princess and the People", BBC video, 1984, (C); "Charles and Diana: The First Decade", BBC Video, 1991, (B); "Diana – The Making of a Princess", ITM Video, 1987, (B).

"Talking Personally" video (companion to the book), ITM Video, 1985, (C), "In Private – In Public video" (companion to the book), ITM Video, 1986, (C).

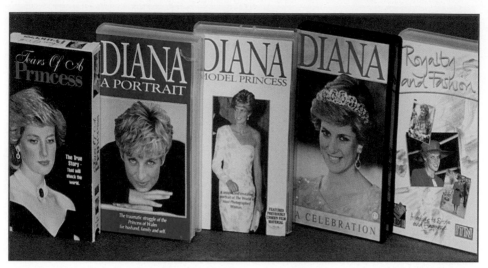

"Tears of a Princess", ITM Video, 1992, (B); "Diana A Portrait", Virgin Video, 1992, (B); "Diana Model Princess", Virgin Video, 1992, (B); "Diana A Celebration", Leisure View Video, 1992, (B); "Royalty and Fashion", ITM Video, 1990, (B).

"Scandals of the Royal Family" video with audiotape, 1993, (C), "Diana and Sarah", Oddyssey Video, 1994, (B); "Diana Queen of Hearts", DD Video, 1996, (B); "Diana A Celebration", Fox Video, 1997, (B); "Diana The People's Princess", ITM Video, 1997, (B); "Diana The People's Princess", MVP Video, 1997, (B).

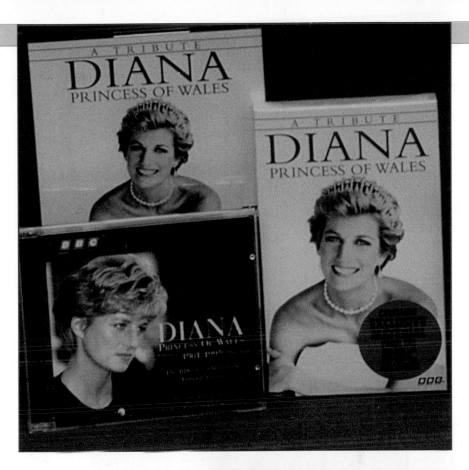

"Diana Princess of Wales" funeral service CD, BBC Music, 1997, (B); "A Tribute" 2-CD set, BBC Audio, 1997, (B); "A Tribute" 2-tape set, BBC Audio, 1997, (B); "Candle in the Wind" CD single, 1997, (A).

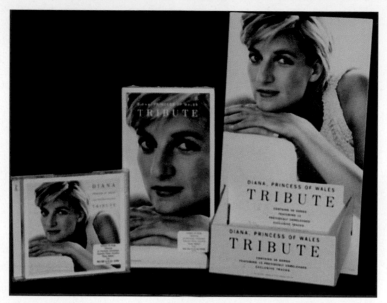

"Diana Tribute" 2-CD set, Sony Music, 1997, (B); "Diana Tribute" 2-tape set, in box, Sony Music, 1997, (B); "Diana Tribute" promotional standee, Sony Music, 1997, (C)

"Diana" interactive video CD-ROM, Compuworks, 1997, (A).

Chapter 5

To Remember Her By

Royal commemoratives have been around since before Queen Victoria, and most royal events are remembered by some sort of commemorative.

Charles and Diana's wedding in 1981 was one of the biggest events of the century, and all kinds of items were issued to mark the occasion.

Usually when commemoratives are issued, several pieces are issued in one style, or one photograph can appear on several different pieces. This means that if a plate to mark the wedding was issued, a mug, vase, or other piece may be issued as well, all bearing the same picture.

In this book, I have tried to show a variety of different things released to commemorate the important events in Diana's life. Commemoratives can be very expensive, and are usually made of china and easily broken.

As with any tourist town, London is filled with commemorative spoons, cookie tins, and other memorabilia on every street corner. I found the small bust of Diana in a London jewelry store and just had to have it, leaving the matching bust of Charles. The paperweights came from the National Gallery of Art in London.

Following Diana's death, commemoratives flooded the market, and as a collector I have been very selective about my purchases.

The candle in the floral box is the first item issued in America that features her memorial funds official logo. In my purchases since her death, I have tried to chose items in good taste which reflect what Diana meant to me and give me something to remember her by.

Charles and Diana Royal Wedding mug, set of two, Arthur Wood, 1981, (C); Charles and Diana mini plate, Finsbury, 1981, (B); Charles and Diana thimble, Finsbury, 1981, (B); Charles and Diana shaving mug (front view), Keystone, 1981, (C).

Ring postcard, one of 60, Prescott Inc., 1981, (C) set; Charles and Diana flute, unknown maker, 1981, (B); engagement postcard, one of 60, Prescott Inc., 1981, (C) set; engagement thimble, St. George China, 1981, (B); Charles and Diana milk glass mug, made in France, 1981, (B).

Royal Wedding bud vase, Keystone, 1981, (C); Charles and Diana mug, made in England, 1981, (B); Royal Wedding plastic commemorative plate, unknown maker, 1981, (B).

Royal Wedding plate, Queen
Anne China, 1981, (C).

Royal Wedding biscuit tin,
Crawford, 1981, mint condition,
(C).

Royal Wedding
plastic flag, made
in England,
1981, (B).

Royal Wedding Irish linen towel, unknown maker, 1981, (B).

Charles and Diana commemorative coin, Royal Mint, 1981, (G); Royal engagement postcard, Kardorama, 1981, (B); Charles and Diana postcard, Colour Master, 1981, (B).

Royal Wedding postcard, one of 60, Prescott Inc., 1981, (C) set; Royal Wedding book, Seymour Press, 1981, (B); Royal Wedding mini plate, Finsbury China, 1981, (B); Royal Wedding thimble, St. George China, 1981, (B); Royal Wedding postcard, one of 60, Prescott, 1981, (C) set.

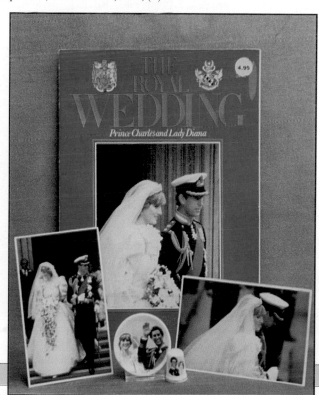

Royal Family postcard series – Diana and William and (far right) Charles, Diana and William, two of 60, 1982, (C) set; Diana and William mini plate, Finsbury, 1983, (B); companion to the mini plate, (B), set of two (C); Diana and William postcard, Pitkin Inc., 1983, (B); Prince William thimble, St. George, 1982, (B).

Charles and Diana mini plate, Weatherby China, 1985, (B); Charles and Diana thimble, unknown maker, 1985, (A); Charles and Diana pillbox, Ashford, 1985, (C); Charles and Diana portrait postcard, Pitkin, 1985, (B).

"Royal Family Group" plate, Finsbury, 1985, (C); "The Royal Family" plate, Finsbury, 1985, (C); Diana and Harry thimble, Finsbury, 1985, (B).

Diana mini bust, Finsbury, 1985, (C); Charles and Diana 10th anniversary thimble, Coverswall, 1991, (C); Diana portrait paperweight, 1991, (C); Diana 30th birthday mug, Coverswall, 1991, (C); Diana spoon, Exquisite Inc., 1982, (C); Diana and Harry thimble, Finsbury, 1984, (B); Diana paperweight, 1982, (C).

Diana commemorative
plate, Staffordshire,
1997, (B).

Diana, Princess of Wales music box, plays "Candle in the Wind", Ardleigh Elliot, 1997, (B).

Princess Diana votive with floating rose candle, Waterford, 1998, (B).

Diana memorial pin with official
logo, Roc Inc., 1998, (B).

Diana, Princess of Wales Memorial Candle,
Slatkin & Co., 1997, (B). This was the first
American item with the Memorial Fund logo.

Chapter 6

It's In The Mail

After Diana's engagement in February 1981, the Royal Mail issued several stamps from commonwealth countries. Most of these were very decorative and featured great artwork.

For her 21st birthday in 1982, the Queen requested that the Royal Mail issue a set of stamps from the commonwealth countries to mark the event. These are shown here with large photos of the Princess and the wedding, and are very sought-after today as a collection.

The Republic of Tonga issued a set of nine stamps following Diana's auction of 79 of her dresses in 1997. These stamps are a much sought-after collectible for Diana fans and stamp collectors.

After her death, stamps were issued from almost every country. The official stamps issued by the Royal Mail in February 1998 were some of the most beautiful. A collectible folder shown here was also sold and is a prize for collectors. The stamps I have shown represent a cross sampling of what is available on the market today.

The post cards pictured here are from a variety of sets and individual cards. Most were purchased on trips to London and when friends visited there.

The black-and-white postcards are very collectible and hard to find.

My favorites are Diana with the Princess Royal and the ones with her children. The face cards are highly collectible and hard to find.

Following her divorce in 1996, Diana's postcards were pulled from the shelves in Britain, but after her death new ones were issued. I'm sure she will become an icon for years to come, and Diana will be in the mail for years to come.

Diana 21st birthday stamps, set of 12, Falkland Islands, Swaziland, Mauritius, (F)

Stamps from Antigua and Barbuda, Bahamas and British Antarctic Territory.

Stamps from Belize, Barbados and Nevis.

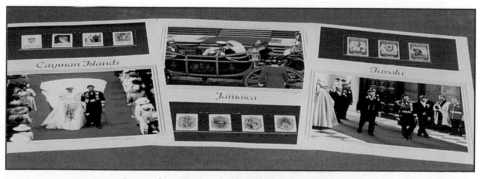

Stamps from the Cayman Islands, Jamaica and Tavalu.

Assorted Royal Wedding stamps from Commonwealth countries, each (A).

Princess Diana Royal gowns stamps from Togo Republic, block of 9 stamps and 9 commemorative sheets of each gown issued after Christies Auction in 1997, set of 10, (B).

Princess Diana 5 x 7 commemorative stamp sheet, Commonwealth of Dominica, 1998, (B); Princess Diana 4 x 6 commemorative stamp sheet, Commonwealth of Dominica, 1998, (A).

Royal Mail stamps with booklet, Royal Mail, 1998, five stamps and booklet, (B).

Tribute stamps of Diana, Princess of Wales by Namibia, 1998, (B).

Select postcards from set of 60 Royal Wedding cards, Prescott, 1981, (C) set.

Select postcards from set of 60 Royal Family cards, 1982, Prescott, (C) set.

Select postcards from set of 30 Charles and Diana in the Antipodes, Prescott, 1983, (C) set.

Set of 10 postcards: "Charles and Diana in Canada", Prescott, 1983, (B) set.

Set of 10 postcards: "Charles and Diana in Australia and America", Prescott, 1985, (B) set.

Assorted 4 x 6 Princess Diana postcards, made in England, 1981 to 1997, each (A).

Assorted 5 x 7 Princess Diana postcards, made in England, 1983 to 1991, each (B).

Assorted 5 x 7 Princess Diana postcards, made in England, 1983 to 1995, each (A).

Assorted Charles and Diana postcards, made in England, 1981 to 1991, each (A).

Assorted Diana and her children postcards, made in England, 1982 to 1991, each (A).

Assorted "Diana and the Royal Family" postcards, made in England, 1986 to 1991, each (B).

Black-and-white postcards, photo cards are Dutch and English, each (B); "sketch" cards are a limited edition of 500, each (B).

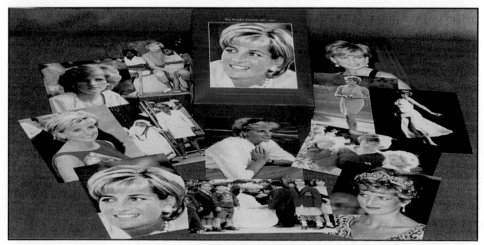

Set of 12 "The People's Princess" commemorative postcards in box with envelopes, WDL Inc., 1997, (B).

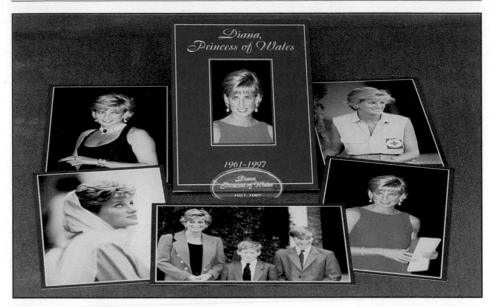

Princess Diana set of five studies in envelope, J. Arthur Dixon, 1997, (B).

Diana "shapes" card (smiling), WPL Inc., 1994, (B); Diana "shapes" card (tiara), WPL Inc., 1994, (B).

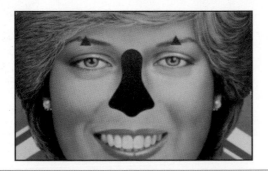

Princess Diana nose card, Hallmark, 1985, (B).

Chapter 7

Plates of a Princess

Plate collecting is one of the top five hobbies in the world, so it wasn't long until Diana, like other icons before her, was immortalized in porcelain.

The Royal Doulton plate was taken from a portrait commissioned in 1987 by Grocers Hall, and still hangs there today. At the time I purchased this triple portrait plate, it was my most expensive item.

In 1989, the Danbury Mint issued their set of six plates and, although they were beautiful, the artist did not know a lot about his subject. The plate entitled "Wedding Portrait" is from a photo of Diana during her 1985 trip to Washington.

After her death in August 1997, the Franklin Mint issued the stunning blue plate with the portrait of Diana wearing her "Elvis" dress (which the Franklin Mint purchased at auction). They began a series of plates on Diana's legacy, five of which are shown here. These plates are some of the best ever produced on Diana and the "Princess of Style" really shows Diana at her best.

Danbury Mint plates, issued 1989 to 1990 by artist Barry Morgan: "Newly Engaged", "Wedding of the Century", "A Future King", "Wedding Portrait", "Flowers for Diana", "Sophisticated Lady"; all plates #A 527.

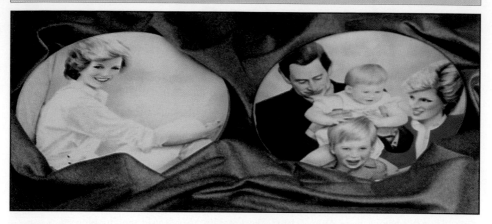

Danbury Mint plates: "Casual Princess", "Family Portrait"; all plates #A 527, complete set of eight (E).

Royal Doulton triple portrait plate, 1991, limited to 10,000, (F).

Diana, Princess of Wales tribute plate, Franklin Mint, by artist Drew Struzan, 1997, limited edition, (B).

Diana "Her Life and Legacy" plates, Franklin Mint, by artist Drew Struzan, 1997 to 1997, (B) each: "Queen of Compassion", "People's Princess", "Angel of Hope", "England's Rose", "Princess of Style".

"The People's Princess", first issue in "Diana, Queen of Our Hearts" plate collection, Bradford Exchange, by artist Jean Monti, (B).

Chapter 8

Day by Day by Day

Calendars are a fun collectible and come in a variety of styles. Diana calendars were a yearly occurrence in the early 1980s: Diana's fashions were the subject of the 1983 calendar and the Royal Family the focus of the years 1985 through 1988, and somehow Diana always had more photos than any other member of the family.

In her native Britain, yearly calendars marked the Royal's year and some were give-aways with magazine subscriptions. Two examples are "1992: The Decade of Diana" and the 1995 "Royal Year" calendar.

Following her death last August, commemorative calendars were out by September, coming from America, Germany, and of course Britain. In most of these cases, money was donated to Diana's charity.

As with magazines, Diana and newspapers go hand in hand. Diana was on the cover of British newspapers almost daily. For this book I have chosen the events in her life, and within that a variety of countries and states to show how globally she was covered.

The *Mirror* titled, "Diana, We'll leave her alone" was from when Diana gave up her public life, and in true tabloid fashion there are about 15 pages of coverage "leaving her alone."

It was a hard decision whether to include the tabloids in this book, but they were a part of her life and although it is a tabloid, the 10th Anniversary issue on Charles and Diana is a keeper.

I hope this chapter gives you a good example of how popular Diana was and her impact day by day.

The Palm Beach Post: 08-31-97, "Diana Dies", (B).

Luxury Lifestyles: Spring 1996, "Royal Scandals", (B); September 1993, "Di Fights Back", (A).

The Globe: 07-30-96, "Di's Divorce Breakdown", (A); August 1997, "Di Makes Love", (A).

The Star: 11-23-93, "Di As You've Never Seen Her Before", (A); 06-30-92, "Di's Cry for Help", (A).

The Star: July 1991, "Charles and Diana's 10th Anniversary, (B); 1993, "Diana & Fergie", (B).

The Enquirer Sunday Review: 09-07-97, "Diana, Queen of Hearts", (B); *Tribune SoundLife*, 09-01-97, "America's Princess, Too", (B).

The Mail on Sunday: 09-07-97, "The Day We All Said Goodbye", (B).

The Post and Courier: 09-05-97, "A Symbol of Style", (A); *The Sun News* Special Section: 09-07-98, "The Life of Princess Diana", (B).

USA Today: September 5 to 7, 1997, "Farewell Diana", (B); 09-01-97, "Death of a Princess", (B).

The New York Times: 09-01-97, "Diana Comes Home to Britain", (A); *The Herald-Sun*: 08-31-97, "Crash Claims Princess Di", (A).

The Sunday Times Style: 01-24-96, "Some Mothers-In-Law Do 'Ave 'Em", (A); *The News Tribune SoundLife*, 06-22-97, "Off the Royal rack", (A).

International Express: February 26 through March 4, 1997, "Diana Pockets Money From Charity Auction", (A); *New York Post*: 06-26-97, "Princess of Sales", (B).

The Sun: 12-10-92, "Throne Alone", (B); *Sunday Mirror*: 04-21-96, "Di: Why I Need A Quickie Divorce", (A).

International Express: March 19 through 25, 1997, "Diana Sparks Church Feud", (A); February 11 through 17, 1997, "Diana's Fury Over Nude Photographs", (A).

Sunday Mirror: 07-14-96, "Princess of Wails", (B); 11-26-95, "Di's Sex Letters Sensation", (A)

The People: 05-24-87, "Diana's Dancing Nights", (A); *International Express*: December 20 through 26, 1995, "Diana and Christopher Whalley", (A).

Daily Mirror: 12-04-93, "Diana – We'll leave her alone", (B).

International Express: November 22 through 28, 1995, "Di-namite", (A); *Sunday Mirror*: 03-10-96, "Di and Hewitt's Sex Secrets", (A).

The Albuquerque Tribune: 07-29-81, "Royal Wedding", (B); *USA Today*: January 27 through 29, 1989, "Diana is Shy Di no more", (A).

"Princess Diana In Remembrance" 1998 calendar, Oliver Books, 1997, (B).

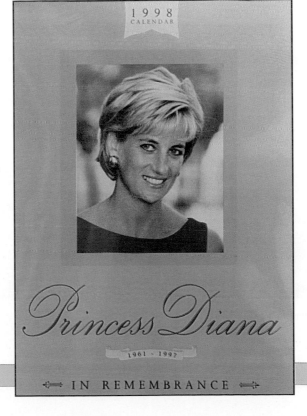

"Diana – The People's Princess" 1998 calendar, PSB Inc., 1997, (B); "Diana" 1998 calendar, Bunte (German), 1997, (B).

1998 commemorative calendar, Portal, 1997, (B); 1998 Diana commemorative calendar, Avalanche, 1997, (B).

"1995 Royalty Calendar", *Royalty Magazine*, 1994, (B); "1997 Royal Moments Calendar" (Diana was January), Jarold, 1996, (B).

"The Wales Family 1991 Calendar", *Royalty Magazine*, 1990, (B); "A Decade of Diana" 1992 multi-language calendar, *Royalty Magazine*, 1991, (B).

"The Royal Family" 1988 calendar, Landmark, 1987, (B); "The Royal Family" 1992 calendar, Landmark, 1991, (B).

"Charles & Diana" 1983 calendar, Cresent, 1982, (B); "Diana Fashion Calendar 1985", Crown Publishers, 1985, (B).

Chapter 9

Rare, Unusual & Hard to Find

In putting this chapter together, I considered the limited availability of the items, such as the press photographs from the AP news wire. Many of these were not published, and due to a connection at the newspaper they were saved from the trash and found a home in my collection.

The press pass from Diana's 1996 trip to Chicago is one of my prized possessions. Only 900 were issued, and I placed an ad in the *Chicago Tribune* and someone sold me theirs.

Among my favorite pieces in my collection are the auction items from the June 25, 1997 auction in New York. From 60,000 catalogs sold, only 1,100 invitations were issued. Half were issued for the main room, and I was very fortunate to get one.

Among the more unusual items are the life-sized standee and the banner from "Diana, Her True Story". Both of these are hard, if not impossible, to find now. The Diana note pad was found during a trip to London in 1987, and was a delight to find.

The *W* magazine cover was a rare find, and now is very sought after by collectors. To have the inside poster intact is an added bonus.

The Ty Beanie Baby "Princess" caused a firestorm when it was issued, and to this day still sells in the hundreds of dollars range. The child's T-shirt was purchased in 1983 and is very unusual, as is the Willie Wear T to commemorate Diana's visit to New York in 1989. It came in the Valentine box shown.

As they continue to age, these items will appreciate in value, as will most Diana collectibles, and only time will tell how rare and hard to find they will become.

Commemorative postcard of the Royal Couple's visit to New Zealand in 1983, Perpetual Trusties, (B); *Daily Mail* Diana binder postcard, unknown maker, 1997, (B).

1985 *W* Magazine cover: "Fashion Victims", came with full-color poster, (B).

Royal Wedding audio postcard which can be played on a phonograph, Radio Tracks Ltd., 1981, (B).

Children's Diana T-shirt, unknown maker, 1983, (B).

Ty "Princess" Beanie Baby, Ty Enterprises, 1997, (D).

Charcoal portrait (11 X 14) of Diana, Murray, 1997, (B).

Linen towel to mark 1981 engagement, Luster, made in England, 1981, (B).

Charles and Diana 3-1/4-inch pewter statue, Stewert, 1982, (B).

Diana key ring with 1991 photo and small bio on back, made in England, 1992, (B); Diana key ring with 1989 photo and small bio on back, made in England, 1992, (B).

Bronze bust by Devine, made in Great Britain, 1982, (C).

Royal family foldout book, printed in England, 1991, (A); Charles,
Diana and William note pad, British, 1983, (A).

Life-size standee of Diana, Princess of Wales,
unknown maker, 1996, (C).

Promotional standee for <u>Diana, Her
True Story</u>, Simon & Schuster, 1992,
(C).

Press pass for the Princess' visit to Chicago in 1996, 900 issued, (D); magnet to commemorate Diana's trip to Chicago, (B); both items are shown with *People* magazine from that time.

Glenn Harvey photograph (8 x 10) taken in 1985 in Australia, (B).

Condolence card from the Princess of Wales on the occasion of her father's death, 1992, (B), shown with *People* magazine.

Majesty magazine's "Royal Wedding Album", printed in England, 1981, (C).

Auction items: gift bag, (A); auction catalog, (C), invitation to main room (B); paddle to bid on dresses, (B).

Promotional poster (18 x 24) to advertise "Keepsake" section of *The Sun News,* 1997, (B).

Portrait of Diana in wedding gown (11 X 14), unknown maker, (B); portrait of Diana (11 X 14), 1982, (B).

"Diana" character note pad, made in England by Fours, 1986, (C).

Diana guide given out free by *Majesty* magazine, 1997, (A).

Greeting card, made in England, 1986, (B); greeting card by Portal American, 1997, (A).

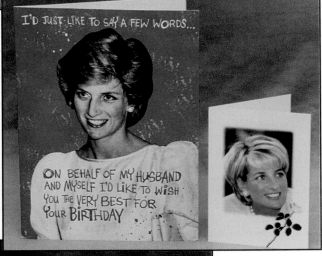

Willie Wear T-shirt to mark Diana's 1989 visit to New York, shown in original heart box, (C).

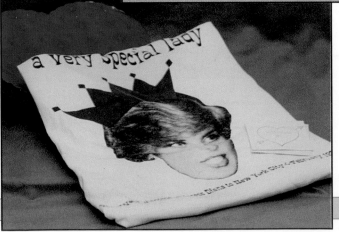

Set of newspaper photographs from Danish News Services, 1990 to 1992, set of 6, (C).

Archive photo and VHS tape from JC Penney covering the Royal visit, 1985, (C).

Display card used in advertising "The Diana Years" from *People*, 1996, (B).

Advertising photo of Diana by Hofmeklers, set of different celebrities, 1984, (B).

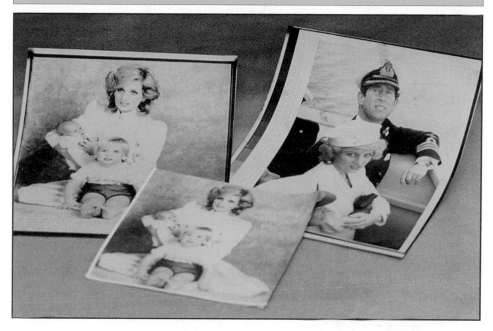

AP Wire photos: Diana, William and Harry, 1984, (B); Charles and Diana in Italy, 1985, (B).

AP Wire photos of Charles and Diana in America, 1985, set of eight, (C).

About the Author

Charles Nobles met Princess Diana in person while on a trip to London in 1992. Even though it was a brief encounter, it was one of the most memorable experiences of his life. He had begun his collection of Diana memorabilia following the Royal Wedding in 1981. The first item in the collection, a commemorative book about the wedding, was a gift from his mother. 17 years later his collection of 2,500 pieces includes items from around the world.

Mr. Nobles and his collection have been in the media numerous times. He was interviewed for *USA Today* and articles about him appeared on the AP Wire service. He was featured on the FX series "Personal FX, The Collectibles Show" as a super collector. He was one of the few chosen to attend the Christies' "Auction of Dresses from the collection of Diana, Princess of Wales."

Mr. Nobles lives in Myrtle Beach, SC, and continues to increase his collection. He plans to donate a portion of the proceeds from this book to Careteam, a local AIDS support organization. He can be contacted at diwatchr@sccoast.net.